IT'S GREAT TO BE A FAN IN
PENNSYLVANIA

by Joanne Mattern

PHILA
21

FOCUS
READERS

www.focusreaders.com

Focus Readers is distributed by North Star Editions:
sales@northstareditions.com | 888-417-0195

Produced for Focus Readers by Red Line Editorial.

Photographs ©: Matt Slocum/AP Images, cover (top), 1 (top); Jeanine Leech/Icon Sportswire/ AP Images, cover (bottom left), 1 (bottom left); Randy Litzinger/Icon Sportswire/AP Images, cover (bottom right), 1 (bottom right); Sean Pavone/Shutterstock Images, 4–5; Valerii Iavtushenko/Shutterstock Images, 7; Red Line Editorial, 9, 29; Jeff Bukowski/Shutterstock Images, 11; Scott Boehm/AP Images, 12–13; John Fisher/Cal Sport Media/AP Images, 15; AP Images, 17; Jeff Roberson/AP Images, 19; Paul Vathis/AP Images, 23; K. Jensen/Shutterstock Images, 24–25; Gene J. Puskar/AP Images, 27; Daniel Zampogna/PennLive.com/AP Images, 30–31; Sarah Crosby/Erie-Times News/AP Images, 33; Ray Stubblebine/AP Images, 35; Don Wright/AP Images, 37; f11photo/Shutterstock Images, 38–39; Aspen Photo/Shutterstock Images, 41; Keith Srakocic/AP Images, 43; Zack Frank/Shutterstock Images, 45

ISBN
978-1-63517-936-1 (hardcover)
978-1-64185-038-4 (paperback)
978-1-64185-240-1 (ebook pdf)
978-1-64185-139-8 (hosted ebook)

Library of Congress Control Number: 2018932003

Printed in the United States of America
Mankato, MN
May, 2018

ABOUT THE AUTHOR

Joanne Mattern has written more than 250 books for children and young adults. Her favorite topics are history, science, sports, and biography. Mattern is a New York native who loves the Yankees. She lives in the Hudson Valley with her husband, four children, and several pets.

TABLE OF CONTENTS

CHAPTER 1

Pennsylvania: A Key Player 5

CHAPTER 2

Pro Teams for All Sports 13

ATHLETE BIO

Wilt Chamberlain 22

CHAPTER 3

College Sports Rule Pennsylvania 25

CHAPTER 4

Pennsylvania's Football Culture 31

ATHLETE BIO

LeSean McCoy 36

CHAPTER 5

Pennsylvania's Passionate People 39

Focus on Pennsylvania • 46

Glossary • 47

To Learn More • 48

Index • 48

PENNSYLVANIA: A KEY PLAYER

When it comes to state pride, Pennsylvanians have a lot to be proud of. Pennsylvania has an amazing history and great places. But when it comes to sports, Pennsylvanians choose sides. All the state's major pro teams are in Pittsburgh or Philadelphia. They are both tough, working-class cities with an intense loyalty to their teams.

Pennsylvania's nickname is the Keystone State. A keystone is a wedge-shaped piece atop an arch.

Pittsburgh Pirates great Roberto Clemente has a bridge named for him near the home of the Pirates.

It locks the other pieces of the arch in place. Pennsylvania's location and important role in building the United States earned it the nickname.

The Pennsylvania **colony** was founded in 1682. The king of England gave the land to Englishman William Penn, even though the region had been home to various American Indian **tribes** for thousands of years. Penn treated the native people fairly and had good relations with them, unlike the leaders in many other North American colonies. But as time went on, Pennsylvania's leaders treated American Indians just as poorly as the leaders of other colonies had.

It was Penn who also founded and named Pennsylvania's capital city. He called it Philadelphia. In Greek, the word *philos* means "love," and *adelphos* means "brother." This is where Philadelphia gets its nickname of the "City

▲ A statue of William Penn stands high atop Philadelphia City Hall.

of Brotherly Love." It is also known simply as "Philly."

By the 1770s, Pennsylvania was at the center of the colonists' fight for independence from Great Britain. In 1776, colonial leaders met in Philadelphia to sign the Declaration of Independence. Later on, the leaders met there again to draft the first US Constitution.

Philadelphia was the center of government throughout the American Revolutionary War (1775–1783). After the United States gained its independence, Philadelphia served as the nation's capital between 1790 and 1800.

Pennsylvania grew thanks in part to its natural resources. The Appalachian Mountains divide the state into two geographic areas. Within Pennsylvania, the Appalachians include subranges called the Allegheny and Pocono Mountains. Many of these mountains have deep deposits of coal and other minerals. These valuable minerals helped make Pennsylvania a leader in mining.

The state has several major waterways. The Delaware River borders Pennsylvania on the east. Other important rivers include the Ohio, Susquehanna, and Monongahela. These rivers provided power and water for mills. They also provided a way to transport cargo to other cities and to ports on the Atlantic Ocean.

Today, nearly 13 million people live in Pennsylvania. The state has several large cities, but Philadelphia and Pittsburgh stand out among the rest in both size and importance. Philadelphia is located on the eastern border of Pennsylvania.

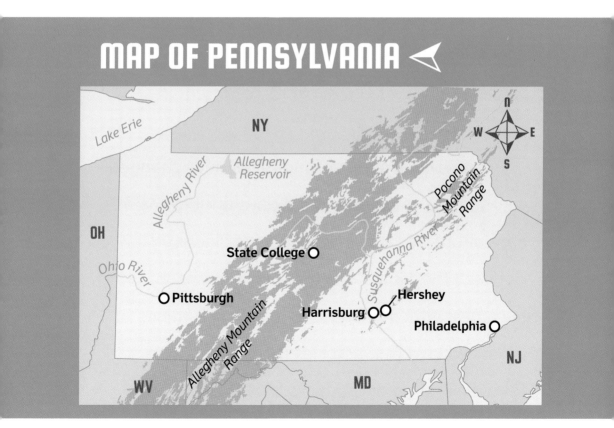

MAP OF PENNSYLVANIA

Lake Erie

NY

Allegheny River

Allegheny Reservoir

Pocono Mountain Range

N
W — E
S

OH

Ohio River

State College ○

Susquehanna River

○ Pittsburgh

Allegheny Mountain Range

Hershey

Harrisburg ○○

Philadelphia ○

WV

MD

NJ

Philadelphia is the second-largest city on the East Coast, and its metropolitan area is home to more than 6 million people. The city has many cultural and historic places to visit, especially for those interested in American history.

Pittsburgh is the second-largest city in Pennsylvania. It is located in the western part of the state. Pittsburgh's metro population is approximately 2 million. Pittsburgh is known as the Steel City because of its history of manufacturing steel.

Pennsylvania's major **industries** have changed over the years. From colonial days until the 1830s, agriculture was the most important industry. Between the 1830s and the 1920s, manufacturing became a vital industry. Pennsylvania's mines produced coal. Its factories made steel, iron, **textiles**, and other products. However, mining

△ The Pittsburgh Steelers logo is based on the "Steelmark" logo representing the steel industry.

and manufacturing became less important during the late 1900s. Today, Pennsylvania has a diverse, modern **economy**. The finance and retail industries are especially important.

The state's history has helped shape its sports teams. And while fans around the state might not always root for the same teams, they root for teams with rich, proud traditions, just like the state itself.

PRO TEAMS FOR ALL SPORTS

Pennsylvania is truly a major league state. It is represented by eight major sports teams and has at least one team in every league.

Baseball was the first professional sport played in Pennsylvania. In 1882, a team known simply as Allegheny began playing in Pittsburgh. After several unsuccessful seasons and several name changes, Allegheny became known as the Pittsburgh Pirates in 1891.

Honus Wagner was one of the first superstars for the Pittsburgh Pirates.

The Pirates have won the World Series five times. They won the 1960 series thanks to a game-winning home run in Game 7 by Bill Mazeroski. That was the only time in the history of Major League Baseball (MLB) that a player ended Game 7 of the World Series with a home run. Perhaps the best player on that team was Hall of Fame outfielder Roberto Clemente. He led the Pirates to another title in 1971. Tragically, he died in a plane crash the following year.

Pittsburgh also holds an important place in the history of the **Negro Leagues**. The Homestead Grays and the Pittsburgh Crawfords both played in Pittsburgh. They featured stars Josh Gibson, Satchel Paige, and James "Cool Papa" Bell.

On the other side of the state, Philadelphia is the home of the Phillies. The team began in 1883 and is the oldest team among all US sports to

▲ Stars Ryan Howard and Jimmy Rollins led the Phillies to their 2008 World Series title.

play in the same city under the same name. The Phillies won the World Series in 1980 and 2008. They have many players inducted in the Hall of Fame, such as slugger Mike Schmidt.

Philadelphia is also home to the only Pennsylvania team in the National Basketball Association (NBA). The 76ers have been members of the NBA since the league's first season in 1949.

Back in those days, they were playing as the Syracuse Nationals. They moved to Philadelphia in 1963. The team then changed its name to the 76ers as a reminder of 1776, the year the Declaration of Independence was signed. During the 1960s, the 76ers featured Wilt Chamberlain, whose incredible scoring ability made him one of basketball's greatest players of all time.

The National Hockey League (NHL) is also popular in Philadelphia. The Philadelphia Flyers came to the city in 1967. The Flyers were the first **expansion team** to win the Stanley Cup, becoming champions in 1974 and 1975. Captain Bobby Clarke led the team during this era.

The Pittsburgh Penguins joined the NHL the same year as the Flyers. The Penguins went on to become one of the best teams in NHL history. Back-to-back championships in 2016 and 2017

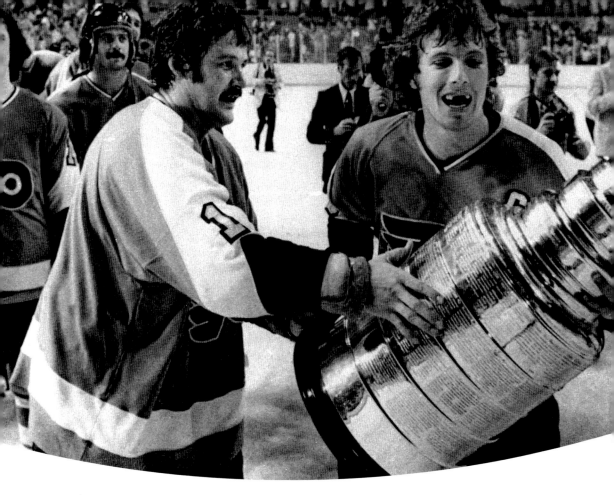

The Flyers teams of the 1970s were known for rough play, earning them the nickname "the Broad Street Bullies."

gave them five total Stanley Cups. That was tied for the fifth-most in NHL history. They got the nickname "Penguins" because their home arena from 1967 to 2010, Civic Arena, was known as "the Igloo."

For parts of three decades, the Penguins' star player was superstar Mario Lemieux. This hockey great and fan favorite scored 100 points or more in 10 different seasons between 1984 and 2006. Carrying on Lemieux's legacy after his retirement was Sidney Crosby. Known as "Sid the Kid," Crosby won the league's Most Valuable Player (MVP) award in just his second season in 2007. He was a key part of returning the Pens to a championship level.

➤ THINK ABOUT IT

Corporations often pay sports teams large amounts of money to have their names on stadiums. Do you think this arrangement benefits the teams and the fans? Why or why not?

Nick Foles threw three touchdowns and even caught one himself to help the Eagles win Super Bowl LII.

Pennsylvanians love all sports, but football is king throughout the state. Philadelphia and Pittsburgh each have a National Football League (NFL) team. The Philadelphia Eagles have been part of the NFL since 1933. But they didn't break through to their first championship until the 2017 season. For much of the season, quarterback Carson Wentz played like an MVP candidate. But he got hurt late in the year. Nick Foles took over.

He led the Eagles to the Super Bowl, where they beat the New England Patriots.

The Pittsburgh Steelers also formed in 1933. In 2008, they won their sixth Super Bowl in their eighth appearance. No other NFL team had won more. The team was originally called the Pirates but was renamed in 1940. "Steelers" references Pittsburgh's long history of manufacturing steel.

The Steelers have always been known for their toughness. They won four Super Bowls in the 1970s with their "Steel Curtain" defense. They were led by lineman "Mean" Joe Greene and linebacker Jack Lambert.

One unique aspect of Pittsburgh's teams is their colors. The city's flag is mostly black and yellow. The Steelers, Pirates, and Penguins all have black and yellow uniforms. Pittsburgh is the only city whose teams all share the same colors.

Pennsylvania's newest pro team plays a different kind of football. Philadelphia Union joined Major League Soccer (MLS) as an expansion team in 2010. Their name refers to the union of the Thirteen Colonies. Meanwhile, their crest includes 13 gold stars and a rattlesnake. The rattlesnake is a reference to a famous political cartoon by longtime Philadelphia resident Benjamin Franklin, published in the 1750s.

WHERE DO THEY PLAY?

Pro Sports Team	Stadium
Philadelphia Phillies	Citizens Bank Park
Pittsburgh Pirates	PNC Park
Philadelphia 76ers	Wells Fargo Center
Philadelphia Union	Talen Energy Stadium
Philadelphia Flyers	Wells Fargo Center
Pittsburgh Penguins	PPG Paints Arena
Philadelphia Eagles	Lincoln Financial Field
Pittsburgh Steelers	Heinz Field

WILT CHAMBERLAIN

Wilt Chamberlain was born in Philadelphia in 1936. He grew to be 7 feet 1 inch (216 cm) tall, earning him the nickname "Wilt the Stilt." Chamberlain went to high school at Overbrook in Philadelphia. He dominated at that level.

Many colleges wanted him to play for them. Chamberlain chose the University of Kansas and led the Jayhawks to the 1957 national title game. Chamberlain was so much better than the other players that rules were changed to slow him down. Teammates used to pass him the ball from out of bounds over the backboard. Chamberlain was so tall and athletic that he easily caught it and scored. The play was soon banned.

In 1959, he signed with his hometown Philadelphia Warriors. The Warriors were founded in 1946 and were original members of the NBA. Chamberlain scored 43 points in his first game.

Wilt Chamberlain's 100-point game remains an all-time NBA record.

It was a sign of things to come. Over his 14-year career, he became the first player to score more than 30,000 points.

Chamberlain's most amazing game occurred on March 2, 1962. Against the New York Knicks, Chamberlain scored an astonishing 100 points. No other NBA player has come close to breaking the record since.

CHAPTER 3

COLLEGE SPORTS RULE PENNSYLVANIA

College sports have unique traditions all their own. Pennsylvania is home to some of the nation's most successful programs. And the teams have some of the most passionate fans in the country.

The state's most beloved college program belongs to Pennsylvania State University. Known simply as Penn State, the Nittany Lions have fans in Pennsylvania and all over the United States.

The Nittany Lion Shrine is a famous landmark on the Penn State campus.

The school boasts 31 **Division I** teams. These teams include baseball, football, and wrestling for men and field hockey and softball for women. Many more sports have teams for both men and women, including basketball, ice hockey, lacrosse, and volleyball.

Of all those teams, there is no question that football is king at Penn State. The school's football stadium holds more than 105,000 people, which makes it one of the largest stadiums in the world. Football games are big events, both on the campus and in the surrounding area. Penn State is a major part of State College, the town in which

> ## ➤ THINK ABOUT IT

Penn State is known for its "sports first" culture. In what ways is that good and bad? Why do you think college sports became such a big part of Penn State's identity?

⬩ When full of fans, Penn State's Beaver Stadium has a larger population than all but three Pennsylvania cities.

the campus is located. People from all over the state come to State College to attend games.

Penn State is one of the most successful programs in the history of college football. The team played its first season in 1887. In 2017, the program surpassed 875 all-time wins. The Nittany Lions also won two national championships in the 1980s. They have produced numerous NFL stars, including Franco Harris and Tamba Hali.

The state's other popular college football program is from the University of Pittsburgh. The Pitt Panthers have won nine national titles, but most of those were before 1940. The Panthers have also had success in men's basketball.

Smaller schools are big in sports as well. The University of Pennsylvania's sports teams are called the Quakers and are especially strong in men's basketball. Villanova University's men's basketball team won national championships in 1985, 2016, and 2018. The Wildcats have also made it to the Final Four several times.

Lehigh University is another well-known Division I sports school. Its wrestling team is notable for its 27 individual national champions and 136 All-Americans. Lehigh's football team has a famous **rivalry** with nearby Lafayette College. The two teams have played against each other since 1884, making it the most-played rivalry in college football. The game is simply called "the Rivalry." It attracts so much attention that on its 150th anniversary in 2014, the game was played at Yankee Stadium in New York City.

PENNSYLVANIA'S DIVISION I COLLEGE FOOTBALL TEAMS

PENNSYLVANIA'S FOOTBALL CULTURE

People in Pennsylvania love sports. And while all sports have their loyal fans, football has its own powerful culture, especially in Pennsylvania's small towns.

Much of Pennsylvania is covered by mountains and valleys. These areas are filled with small towns. Many of these towns depended on coal mines and steel mills for jobs. But in recent years, those industries have started to decline.

Schools such as Pittsburgh's Central Catholic dream of winning the state championship.

Thousands of people lost their jobs. That had a huge negative impact on the state's economy. Some parts of Pennsylvania are still going through hard times. But sports can be a way to express pride in the communities.

One of the most popular ways to pass the time in Pennsylvania's small towns is to go to high school football games. In some towns, it is one of the only forms of entertainment on Friday nights. And for the athletes, it is one of the only activities.

Athletes and coaches work hard to make their school teams the best. Residents support the teams by going to games and making the players feel like heroes. The culture of supporting a winning team makes people feel good—not just about themselves, but also their hometown.

Pride is on the line when one team plays another. And some of these rivalries go back

Big crowds are common at Pennsylvania high school football games.

a long time. Penn Charter and Germantown Academy have played every year since 1887. Many football historians believe it is the longest uninterrupted rivalry in the nation.

One of Philadelphia's Thanksgiving traditions is a football game. Northeast High School and Central High School battle for the Wooden Horse trophy each year. The rivalry dates back to 1892.

Perhaps because of Pennsylvania's strong love of football, the state has produced a number of professional players. This is especially true in the western Pennsylvania hills. That part of the state has produced some of football's all-time great quarterbacks. They include Johnny Unitas, Jim Kelly, Joe Montana, Dan Marino, Joe Namath, and George Blanda. All of them are in the Pro Football Hall of Fame. And the local heroes who

➤ THINK ABOUT IT

Which high school sports are popular in your town? Why do you think that's the case?

⬆ Prior to his NFL success, Dan Marino was a standout quarterback in Pittsburgh both in high school and college.

go on to make it big often remember their roots. Jim Kelly, for example, donated a large amount of **memorabilia** to his hometown of East Brady.

Through the 2017 season, Pennsylvania has produced the fifth-most NFL players of all the states. But it has produced the most Pro Football Hall of Famers. Thirty-three of these all-time great players came from the Keystone State.

LESEAN MCCOY

LeSean McCoy was a Pennsylvania football star from high school all the way to the pros. Born in 1988 in Harrisburg, he became a star running back at Bishop McDevitt High School. During his junior year, McCoy rushed for more than 2,800 yards and scored 30 touchdowns. He was ranked as the No. 1 high school player in the country.

McCoy broke his ankle during his last high school game. But the injury inspired him to work even harder. After his recovery, he went on to play at the University of Pittsburgh. There, he rushed for more than 2,700 yards and 35 touchdowns in two seasons. As one of the best running backs in the country, he decided to turn pro rather than finish college.

The Philadelphia Eagles chose McCoy in the second round of the 2009 NFL Draft. He was the Eagles' starting running back from 2010 until

▲ LeSean McCoy was a standout running back for the Pittsburgh Panthers.

2015. McCoy led the NFL in rushing yards in 2013, and he became the Eagles' all-time leading rusher after the 2014 season.

McCoy was traded to the Buffalo Bills in 2015, and he remained a great player there. His 1,138 yards in 2017 helped the Bills make the playoffs for the first time in 18 years.

PENNSYLVANIA'S PASSIONATE PEOPLE

Pennsylvania is historic. It played a key part in the history of the United States. The state's history has included challenges, but the people of Pennsylvania have always overcome those challenges. That tough, fighting spirit is a big part of the identity of Pennsylvania's teams.

For sports fans, games become even more exciting when a rivalry is involved. Some of Pennsylvania's best rivalries are within the state.

The Liberty Bell in Philadelphia is an iconic piece of American history.

For many years, the biggest rivalry in Pennsylvania was the one between Penn State and Pitt. The two schools first played each other in football in 1893. As the two most prominent football programs in Pennsylvania, the rivalry gained steam quickly. The teams did not play from 1999 through 2015, but they renewed the rivalry in 2016. Other college rivalries in the state include Lehigh University and Lafayette College, and Penn State and Temple University.

Rivalries exist in professional sports as well. The Philadelphia Eagles and the Pittsburgh Steelers are rivals in football. Meanwhile, the Philadelphia Flyers and the Pittsburgh Penguins are rivals in hockey, while the Philadelphia Phillies and the Pittsburgh Pirates are rivals in baseball. Many Pennsylvania sports rivalries come down to Philadelphia versus Pittsburgh.

⯅ Football may rule Pennsylvania, but basketball is the most popular sport at Temple University.

The two cities have a unique relationship due to their locations in the far eastern and far western parts of the state. Because they are so far apart, each city is the most important city on its side of the state. This situation has allowed both cities to grow and prosper in their own ways.

Philadelphia and Pittsburgh have some things in common, but they grew into very different cities. Philadelphia is huge with tall skyscrapers.

Pittsburgh, on the other hand, has a reputation as a tough, working-class city. It is not glamorous, and its residents are proud of that fact.

The two cities also have rivalries with teams in other states. The Pittsburgh Steelers have a longtime rivalry with the Cleveland Browns. Both teams are among the oldest in the NFL. The rivalry was especially intense in the 1970s.

Philadelphia also has many rivalries with New York City, as they are the two biggest cities on the East Coast. The Eagles and New York Giants have been rivals since the Eagles joined the NFL in 1933. The Giants welcomed them to the league by beating them 56–0. Other Philadelphia–New York rivalries include the Phillies and Mets in baseball and the Flyers and Rangers in hockey.

Passionate fans don't exist just at the top levels. Pennsylvania is also home to numerous

Pittsburghers are very proud of their city, especially when the Steelers are playing.

professional minor league teams in a variety of sports. In fact, Harrisburg has been named one of the best cities for minor league sports.

Pennsylvania's capital city is home to the Hershey Bears, the top minor league **farm team** of the NHL's Washington Capitals. The Bears are the oldest professional hockey team not playing in the NHL. The Washington Nationals also have a minor league team in Harrisburg called the Harrisburg Senators, two levels below the majors.

Harrisburg and other cities also have professional teams in lesser-known sports, such as rugby and roller derby.

As if Pennsylvanians couldn't get enough football, the state has two arena football teams. The Soul play in the Arena Football League in Philadelphia. Meanwhile, the Lehigh Valley Steelhawks play in the National Arena League in Allentown. Legendary Eagles quarterback Ron Jaworski is the Soul's majority owner.

Because some of these teams represent smaller cities, they might be the only game in town. Fans there are passionate to have a team

> THINK ABOUT IT

How can rivalries make sports more exciting? Can they also cause trouble? If so, how?

⬆ The Hershey Bears' former home of Hersheypark Arena is where Wilt Chamberlain scored 100 points in a game.

that represents them. They might root for a major league team in another city, but it's always more fun to have a hometown team to cheer for.

Pennsylvania sees itself as ready for anything. It's a place—and a people—that has faced problems, made history, and come out on top. For Pennsylvania, sports are a perfect part of that tough and historic image.

FOCUS ON
PENNSYLVANIA

Write your answers on a separate piece of paper.

1. Write a sentence that describes why sports are so important in small towns, as discussed in Chapter 4.

2. Which is your favorite Pennsylvania sports team? Why?

3. Which was the first professional sports team in Pennsylvania?

     A. Pittsburgh Steelers
     B. Philadelphia Phillies
     C. Pittsburgh Pirates

4. Why is there a rivalry between Philadelphia and Pittsburgh?

     A. The two cities are very close to each other.
     B. The cities have different backgrounds.
     C. Both cities have more than one sports team.

Answer key on page 48.

GLOSSARY

colony
An area controlled by a country that is far away.

Division I
The top level of college sports in the United States.

economy
A system of goods, services, money, and jobs.

expansion team
A new team that is added to a league.

farm team
A minor league team that develops players for a major league team.

industries
Types of business that many companies are involved in.

memorabilia
Objects kept or collected because of historical interest.

Negro Leagues
Baseball leagues for black players. The leagues existed because black athletes were not allowed to play in Major League Baseball until the late 1940s.

rivalry
An ongoing competition between two players or teams.

textiles
Cloth made by knitting or weaving.

tribes
Groups of people that share a common heritage.

TO LEARN MORE

BOOKS

Evdokimoff, Natasha. *Pennsylvania: The Keystone State.*
New York: AV2 by Weigl, 2016.

Hall, Brian. *Sidney Crosby: Hockey Star.* Mendota Heights,
MN: North Star Editions, 2018.

Whiting, Jim. *Philadelphia 76ers.* Mankato, MN: Creative
Education, 2018.

NOTE TO EDUCATORS

Visit **www.focusreaders.com** to find lesson plans,
activities, links, and other resources related to this title.

INDEX

Chamberlain, Wilt, 16,
22–23

Harrisburg Senators,
43

Hershey Bears, 43

Lafayette College, 28,
40

Lehigh University, 28,
40

Lehigh Valley
Steelhawks, 44

McCoy, LeSean, 36–37

Penn State, 25–27, 40

Philadelphia 76ers,
15–16

Philadelphia Eagles,
19–20, 36–37, 40,
42, 44

Philadelphia Flyers,
16–17, 40, 42

Philadelphia Phillies,
14–15, 40, 42

Philadelphia Soul, 44

Philadelphia Union, 21

Pittsburgh Penguins,
16–18, 20, 40

Pittsburgh Pirates,
13–14, 20, 40

Pittsburgh Steelers,
20, 40, 42

Temple University, 40

University of
Pennsylvania, 28

University of
Pittsburgh, 28, 36

Villanova University,
28

Answer Key: **1.** Answers will vary; **2.** Answers will vary; **3.** C; **4.** B